Take Good Care of My World!

The Story of Adam and Eve in the Garden

We are grateful to the following team of authors for their contributions to *God Loves Me*, a Bible story program for young children. This Bible story, one of a series of fifty-two, was written by Patricia L. Nederveld, managing editor for CRC Publications. Suggestions for using this book were developed by Sherry Ten Clay, training coordinator for CRC Publications and freelance author from Albuquerque, New Mexico. Yvonne Van Ee, an early childhood educator, served as project consultant and wrote God Loves Me, the program guide that accompanies this series of Bible storybooks.

Nederveld has served as a consultant to Title I early childhood programs in Colorado. She has extensive experience as a writer, teacher, and consultant for federally funded preschool, kindergarten, and early childhood programs in Colorado, Texas, Michigan, Florida, Missouri, and Washington, using the High/Scope Education Research Foundation curriculum. In addition to writing the Bible Footprints church school curriculum for four- and five-year-olds, Nederveld edited the revised *Threes* curriculum and the first edition of preschool through second grade materials for the *LiFE* curriculum, all published by CRC Publications.

Ten Clay taught preschool for ten years in public schools in California, Missouri, and North Carolina and served as a Title IV preschool teacher consultant in Kansas City. For over twenty-five years she has served as a church preschool leader and also as a MOPS (Mothers of Preschoolers) volunteer. Ten Clay is coauthor of the preschool-kindergarten materials of the *LiFE* curriculum published by CRC Publications.

Van Ee is a professor and early childhood program advisor in the Education Department at Calvin College, Grand Rapids, Michigan. She has served as curriculum author and consultant for Christian Schools International and wrote the original Story Hour organization manual and curriculum materials for fours and fives.

Photos on page 5 and 20: SuperStock.

Library of Congress Cataloging-in-Publication Data

Nederveld, Patricia L., 1944-
    Take good care of my world!: the story of Adam and Eve in the garden/
Patricia L. Nederveld.
       p. cm. — (God loves me; bk. 4)
    Summary: Simply retells how Adam and Eve cared for all of God's creation.
Includes follow-up activities.
    ISBN 1-56212-273-8
    1. Creation—Juvenile literature. 2. Ecology—Religious aspects—
Christianity—Juvenile literature. 3. Adam (Biblical figure)—Juvenile
literature. 4. Eve (Biblical figure)—Juvenile literature. 5. Bible stories,
English—O.T. Genesis. [1. Human Ecology—Religious aspects—Christianity.
2. Adam (Biblical figure) 3. Eve (Biblical figure) 4. Bible stories—O.T.]
I. Title. II. Series: Nederveld, Patricia L., 1944- God loves me; bk. 4.
BS1199.C57N44 1998
222'.1109505—dc21
                                              97-37043
                                                CIP
                                                    AC

Take Good Care of My World!

The Story of Adam and Eve in the Garden

PATRICIA L. NEDERVELD

ILLUSTRATIONS BY CATHY ANN JOHNSON

CRC Publications
Grand Rapids, Michigan

This is a story
from God's
book, the Bible.

It's for say name(s) of
your child(ren).
It's for me too!

Genesis 1:28;
2:18-20

I wonder if you know the name of this animal?

And this one?

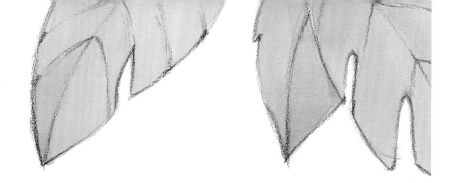

And this one?

Do you know who gave each one of God's creatures its very own name?

A dam did! God gave that job to Adam. And Adam gave every animal, every bird, and every fish a special name of its very own.

When Adam finished that job, God had more work for Adam and Eve to do. "My world is for you to enjoy," God told them. "Please

take good care of all the animals, birds, and fish! Take good care of the trees and flowers too. And enjoy each delicious fruit and vegetable. I made them for you."

Adam and Eve remembered God's words: "Take good care of my world!" They loved God's beautiful world. And they took very good care of every animal, every bird, and every fish.

Every day Adam and Eve obeyed God's words: "Take good care of my world!" They took very good care of each tree and bush, every flower and patch of grass.

Adam and Eve did a good job of taking care of God's world. And when they were finished each day, can you guess what they did?

Yes! M-m-m-m. It was delicious!

When God looked around at the beautiful new world and all that was in it, the world looked very good.

Yes, it *was* very good! Adam and Eve took very good care of everything! God was happy.

I wonder if *you* want to help take care of God's world too . . .

Dear God, thank you for giving us such a wonderful world. We want to take good care of everything in it. Amen.

Suggestions for Follow-up

Opening

As you welcome your little ones, help them find familiar things in your room. You might point out the snapshots of the children hanging on the door or wall or an art project created by the group. Recall a happy memory from last time.

As you gather the children around you, tell them how much God loves them. Invite them to think about what they saw outside as they came today. Name each child and marvel with them that God made the trees, flowers, birds, grass, and sky for each one of them.

Learning Through Play

Learning through play is the best way! The following activity suggestions are meant to help you provide props and experiences that will invite the children to play their way into the Scripture story and its simple truth. Try to provide plenty of time for the children to choose their own activities and to play individually. Use group activities sparingly—little ones learn most comfortably with a minimum of structure.

1. Before the children arrive, wad up pieces of newspaper and hide each piece around the room. Tell the children that you have hidden trash (show them a paper wad) all over the room. Provide large paper grocery bags for collecting the newspaper. Children will enjoy finding the hidden trash and throwing it into the bag. They might want to hide it all again and repeat the game.

2. In your art center, set out large crayons and sidewalk chalk. Give each child a paper lunch bag, and encourage children to scribble on the bags with the crayons and chalk. Label each bag with these words: [name] takes care of God's world. Explain that this bag can be used for trash in the car or at home.

3. Enjoy a walk around a small part of God's world. To keep your little ones safe, use a long jump rope as a walking rope. Have one adult at each end of the rope, and show children how to hold onto the rope with one hand. As you walk together, talk about taking care of God's world, and notice things your little ones can do (water flowers, plant seeds, pull weeds, gather leaves, pick up trash). Depending on the season of the year, stop to do one activity.

4. Plant beans or other quick-growing seeds in a paper cup. Show your little planters how to water their seeds with one or two teaspoons of water each day.

5. Sorting is a favorite activity for your little ones. Find several kinds of trash that can be recycled in your community. (Make sure these recyclables have no sharp edges or harmful liquids.) Furnish large containers—cardboard boxes or laundry baskets—for sorting. Talk about keeping God's world clean and beautiful.

6. Cut out a simple tree shape for each child from green construction paper. Give each child a shallow container of colored cereal. Using white glue, dot each tree several times with

glue. Children can place cereal on each dot—and enjoy a snack too. Talk about the good food that grows in God's beautiful world.

7. Set out beautiful objects (leaves, flowers, pinecones, stones, gourds, garden vegetables, fruits, and the like) from God's world for children to touch and admire. Notice the shapes and colors. Help children remember God's words to Adam and Eve: "Take good care of my world."

Closing

As you prepare to say goodbye, begin singing quietly "God Is So Good" (Songs Section, *God Loves Me* program guide). Repeat the words several times as children join in. Add these words for a second stanza:

> *I love God's world,*
> *I love God's world,*
> *I love God's world,*
> *He's so good to me.*

Read the prayer on page 21 again. As your little ones leave, remind them to help take care of God's world.

At Home

We can all care for God's world. Filling, dumping, sorting, and imitating are fun for young children. You can use these activities to involve your little one as you do chores around the house and yard. Your child will love to copy your earthkeeping ideas. Remember that the best teacher of all is your example of love for God's world.

Old Testament Stories

Blue and Green and Purple Too! *The Story of God's Colorful World*

It's a Noisy Place! *The Story of the First Creatures*

Adam and Eve *The Story of the First Man and Woman*

Take Good Care of My World! *The Story of Adam and Eve in the Garden*

A Very Sad Day *The Story of Adam and Eve's Disobedience*

A Rainy, Rainy Day *The Story of Noah*

Count the Stars! *The Story of God's Promise to Abraham and Sarah*

A Girl Named Rebekah *The Story of God's Answer to Abraham*

Two Coats for Joseph *The Story of Young Joseph*

Plenty to Eat *The Story of Joseph and His Brothers*

Safe in a Basket *The Story of Baby Moses*

I'll Do It! *The Story of Moses and the Burning Bush*

Safe at Last! *The Story of Moses and the Red Sea*

What Is It? *The Story of Manna in the Desert*

A Tall Wall *The Story of Jericho*

A Baby for Hannah *The Story of an Answered Prayer*

Samuel! Samuel! *The Story of God's Call to Samuel*

Lions and Bears! *The Story of David the Shepherd Boy*

David and the Giant *The Story of David and Goliath*

A Little Jar of Oil *The Story of Elisha and the Widow*

One, Two, Three, Four, Five, Six, Seven! *The Story of Elisha and Naaman*

A Big Fish Story *The Story of Jonah*

Lions, Lions! *The Story of Daniel*

New Testament Stories

Jesus Is Born! *The Story of Christmas*

Good News! *The Story of the Shepherds*

An Amazing Star! *The Story of the Wise Men*

Waiting, Waiting, Waiting! *The Story of Simeon and Anna*

Who Is This Child? *The Story of Jesus in the Temple*

Follow Me! *The Story of Jesus and His Twelve Helpers*

The Greatest Gift *The Story of Jesus and the Woman at the Well*

A Father's Wish *The Story of Jesus and a Little Boy*

Just Believe! *The Story of Jesus and a Little Girl*

Get Up and Walk! *The Story of Jesus and a Man Who Couldn't Walk*

A Little Lunch *The Story of Jesus and a Hungry Crowd*

A Scary Storm *The Story of Jesus and a Stormy Sea*

Thank You, Jesus! *The Story of Jesus and One Thankful Man*

A Wonderful Sight! *The Story of Jesus and a Man Who Couldn't See*

A Better Thing to Do *The Story of Jesus and Mary and Martha*

A Lost Lamb *The Story of the Good Shepherd*

Come to Me! *The Story of Jesus and the Children*

Have a Great Day! *The Story of Jesus and Zacchaeus*

I Love You, Jesus! *The Story of Mary's Gift to Jesus*

Hosanna! *The Story of Palm Sunday*

The Best Day Ever! *The Story of Easter*

Goodbye—for Now *The Story of Jesus' Return to Heaven*

A Prayer for Peter *The Story of Peter in Prison*

Sad Day, Happy Day! *The Story of Peter ad Dorcas*

A New Friend *The Story of Paul's Conversion*

Over the Wall *The Story of Paul's Escape in a Basket*

A Song in the Night *The Story of Paul and Silas in Prison*

A Ride in the Night *The Story of Paul's Escape on Horseback*

The Shipwreck *The Story of Paul's Rescue at Sea*

Holiday Stories

Selected stories from the New Testament to help you celebrate the Christian year

Jesus Is Born! *The Story of Christmas*

Good News! *The Story of the Shepherds*

An Amazing Star! *The Story of the Wise Men*

Hosanna! *The Story of Palm Sunday*

The Best Day Ever! *The Story of Easter*

Goodbye—for Now *The Story of Jesus' Return to Heaven*

These fifty-two books are the heart of *God Loves Me,* a Bible story program designed for young children. Individual books (or the entire set) and the accompanying program guide *God Loves Me* are available from CRC Publications (1-800-333-8300).